Houses and Homes

Contents

	Page

written by Pam Holden

1

Some homes are made of logs.
This house is a log cabin.
It is on a mountain.

log cabin

Some houses are built of stone.
This home is a castle.
It is in a forest.

castle

Some houses are made
of bricks.
This home is a farmhouse.
It is in the country.

farmhouse

Some houses are built of wood.
This home is a treehouse.
It is in the jungle.

treehouse

Some homes are made of mud.
This house is a hut.
It is in the desert.

hut

Some homes go on the water.
This is a houseboat.
It goes on a river.

houseboat

Some homes have wheels.
This is a trailer home.
It goes on the road.

trailer home

igloo

Some homes are made of snow.
This house is an igloo. Brrr!